Letters From Home

by

Salvatore LoGiudice

Printed by Lulu.com

First Printing 1998 Serialized in P-Town Scene Magazine
Issues 1-10. Written by Salvatore LoGiudice as John Cloud.

Second Printing August 2007 Novel Format at Lulu.com

Third Printing May 2008 Novel Format at Lulu.com

ISBN: 978-0-6152-1086-5

In memory of
John and Jean Fuchko
and
For Mom

"Tolerance and acceptance is as much for ourselves as for others."

LETTER 01

Dear William,

Thank you so much for your last letter. You are the only one in the family that seems to have time for this old lady.

I've been thinking quite a bit about your announcement at the family reunion, and I don't know why everyone is in such an uproar about it. I suppose they're upset that you

needed to move all the way to Provincetown
Rhode Island just to do those drag racing
shows of yours. That is what you do, isn't it?
I've spoken to your Grandfather about it, and
what a story he has come up with! I am very
worried. I think he may be going senile. I
suppose if that is where the drag showing is
happening, then you have to be there. But
really! Rhode Island!

Things here are going as well as can be
expected. Your Grandfather was mowing the
lawn the other day and that awful paperboy of
ours threw the daily right in front of the
machine. What a mess it made! I rushed out
to scold the boy, but he just rode away
laughing. It made me so mad!

Everything seems fine, but I know there is
trouble coming. I can feel it in my bones.
Your mother doesn't seem happy with her
job, and your younger brother keeps talking
about wanting a tattoo. I hope he doesn't get
one…it will make me so sad. I told him so
and he just got angry.

Oh, William I miss you so much. You were
always the one who spent time with me, now
it seems everyone is too busy or just doesn't
care. I'm sorry, I don't mean to sound blue.
Everything is just fine.

What a storm we had! It was raining cats and
dogs! Of course, that is only an expression.

Will close for now. William, please write to
me. I enjoy your letters so much.

Love,
Gram
P.S. May god bless and keep you.

Letters From Home

<u>LETTER 02</u>

Dear William,

Thank you so much for your last letter. You are the only one in the family that seems to have time for this old lady.

I was so happy when I got your last letter, that I stood right on the street reading it. Mrs. Babcock, the widow from up the street, rode past in her new station wagon and beeped. It nearly scared me to death! You know she has eyes for your Grandfather, but I was polite as always and waved back to her.

Your Grandfather and I got into quite an argument over your last letter. I just knew that Provincetown was the capital of Rhode Island, but he said no. After quite a lengthy discussion, (you know how pig headed he can be) I pulled out the atlas that came with those encyclopedias we bought for your uncle when he wanted to go to college on the GI bill. Imagine my surprise! You'll notice that I addressed this letter to Provincetown Massachusetts, I hope it arrives all right, since everyone thinks Provincetown is in Rhode Island.

 I'm not sure I understand your job as you explained it in your last letter. I thought drag racing involved automobiles. Obviously you must be very good at it, since you've already been promoted to drag racing queen. I am so proud of you!

We are still having trouble with that awful paperboy of ours. He just throws the daily any old place. Yesterday I had to fish it out of the forsythia bushes. Your Grandfather wants to call his editor, but I won't let him. He *is* just a boy afterall!

We will be going to your brother's birthday party this Saturday, and we are very concerned. He still wants that tattoo, and the whole family is in an uproar about it. I've told your mother to put her foot down about it, but she won't listen to me. No one ever does.

Will close for now. William, please write to me. I enjoy your letters so much.

Love,
Gram
P.S. May god bless and keep you.
P.P.S. Everything is just fine.

Letters From Home

LETTER 03

Dear William,

Thank you so much for your last letter. You are the only one in the family that seems to have time for this old lady.

Will this dreary weather ever end? It has been raining for days and it makes me feel so blue.

Your Brother's birthday party was very nice. His friends all seemed like fine young people, even though they all had tattoos and one had an earring in his nose! The music was a little loud, and your Grandfather and I had to go lie down after a while, but we all had a fine time. It was really very nice. I'm not just saying that.

After the young folks went off to have their young folks party, we adults all sat at the table over coffee. I told them all that you had already been promoted to Drag Racing *Queen*. You should have seen the look of shock on their faces! Your Grandfather tried to hush me, but I am so proud! I always knew you were special. So handsome and talented! Remember how well you learned to sew?

I've never told you this before, but I think back to those days when you and I would work along side each other to prepare the Sunday meal. Remember how I always tried to get you to go out and play with the boys? But you never did, you always stayed at my side. How I miss that! Seems to be so little to look forward to these days.

I'm sorry. Please forgive me. I don't mean to sound so sad. Everything is just fine.

Your Grandfather explained to me that you are gay, and I am glad. You deserve to be happy! You are such a fine young man, and so neat and tidy! You'll make some special girl a perfect husband. Most boys your age are so sloppy!

Will close for now. William, please write to me. I enjoy your letters so much.

Love,
Gram
P.S. May god bless and keep you.

Letters From Home

LETTER 04

Dear William,

Thank you so much for your last letter. You are the only one in the family that seems to have time for this old lady.

I cried and cried when I got your last letter. I just don't know what to do. I always thought it was strange that the news made such a big deal about gay people. I thought it meant you were all happy for no reason. Those parades all seemed so festive and fun. I hope you are not angry with me William, I just don't know what to say about it. I cannot speak to anyone, not even the family about this. I don't know how they'll take it. Perhaps I can work up the nerve to discuss it with your Grandfather, and maybe he'll know what we can do to help.

Well, your brother's done it! He's gotten a tattoo! It looks like a skull, of all things, and it's just awful! He is so proud of it though, and we want to seem supportive of him. I told him it was lovely, and silently asked God to forgive me this one tiny lie. Of course I'll have to spend an extra day in purgatory for it, but I don't mind.

Your Grandfather has gone to war with the paperboy. He refused to pay for the daily the boy threw into the lawnmower, and the boy was mad! He said he wouldn't deliver the paper anymore if we didn't pay for it, and your Grandfather told him that if he didn't deliver the paper, that he would call the boy's editor. You wouldn't have believed the argument I overheard. I never expected such language from your Grandfather!

Oh, William. I don't know what I'm going to do. Mrs. Babcock rode past again in her shiny new station wagon while your Grandfather and I were working in the front garden. You should have seen the gleam in her eye when she looked at your Grandfather. He doesn't believe me, but I just know she's going to try something soon.

Still, everything's fine. I don't mean to worry you. I'm sure your days are full trying to be gay and all, it's just that I miss you so much. Everything is perfectly fine. I'm not just saying that.

Will close for now. William, please write to me. I enjoy your letters so much.

Love,
Gram
P.S. May god bless and keep you.

Letters From Home

LETTER 05

Dear William,

Thank you so much for your last letter. You are the only one in the family that seems to have time for this old lady.

I tried to speak to your Grandfather about your problem, but I just couldn't work up the nerve. I know he loves you too, but even after 49 years of marriage, I just don't know how to

talk to him about it. I guess I don't
understand. Why do you want to be gay? Are
your friends trying to make you do it? I know
how difficult it can be when friends push you
to do something you don't want to do. You
just tell them no, and everything will be fine,
believe me. I just know if you stand up for
yourself, you'll be so much happier.

Do you remember how upset I was when Phil
Donohue went off the air? Well, that was
nothing compared to how I felt when Mrs.
Babcock asked your Grandfather and I to
dinner. I didn't want to go, but your
Grandfather said that we shouldn't be rude.

She took us to the House of Wang, a little
oriental restaurant next to the K-mart. I was
very surprised at how nice everything was.
Mr. Wang was very gracious, and laid to rest
my fears about eating cat. He said it was just a
fable. I didn't understand him at first, since
Mr. Wang has such a heavy accent. I don't
think your Grandfather understood him at all.
He just kept smiling at Mr. Wang and
nodding.

Mrs. Babcock seemed very nice throughout
the whole meal, and even insisted that she pay
for everything. Of course we wouldn't let her.
Perhaps she was on her best behavior because

she knew I was onto her. Her car was very nice, and we enjoyed the ride very much. It has what they call power windows, and your Grandfather kept rolling them up and down until I put a stop to it. He pretended that he was just concerned that the wind not muss my hair, but I knew better. He liked playing with all the gadgets. You know how he is about that sort of thing. He has started talking about getting a new car, but they are so dear! I'm not sure we can afford it.

Money is tight as always. But we get by. Everything is fine here. Not a thing to worry about.

Will close for now. William, please write to me. I enjoy your letters so much.

Love,
Gram
P.S. May god bless and keep you.

Letters From Home

LETTER 06

Dear William,

Thank you so much for your last letter. You are the only one in the family that seems to have time for this old lady.

I've done a bad thing. Your last letter got me thinking, and so, foolish old lady that I am, I went to speak with Reverend Wilson about it. I explained to him that you were a gay drag racing queen, and that it was just like your hair color. He told me that you were in league with the devil, and that I should cut you out of the family unless you changed your sinful ways!

I informed him that gluttony was as much of a sin as any, and that perhaps he should think about losing a few pounds before he went around trying to take slivers out of his brother's eyes! He made me so mad! I told him that we wouldn't be attending services anymore, since our Grandson was not welcome! I even told him to take his ideas about the devil and put them right in his patootie! You are my Grandson, and I love you no matter what.

Your Grandfather thinks I may have gone too far with the patootie comment, but he could tell I was angry and let the subject drop for a while. We did finally talk about it some, and we've decided to support you in being as gay as you'd like. Now you must be honest with us, does it cost extra being gay? I'm sure it does. You know we don't have much left once the bills are paid, but what we have is yours! Please let us know how much you need to be a little more gay and we'll send you a check right away!

Now, I'm being honest with you, and I expect you to be honest with me. Since I said such mean things to Reverend Wilson and I'm sure I will spend so much more time in purgatory for it, especially after the patootie comment, I cannot afford to tell any more little white lies now. (I hope your brother doesn't ask me if I like his tattoo again!) I don't know if being gay is a sin or not. I suppose if God made you into a gay, then it must be part of His design. If it is a sin, then He will forgive you just as He forgives me my little white lies (even though they *are* intended to protect other people's feelings) and even Reverend Wilson will be forgiven for his gluttony.

You are a kind and loving young man, and we believe that the Good Lord will judge you based upon that. Your Grandfather and I are very proud of you! You must never forget that.

Will close for now. William, please write to me. I enjoy your letters so much.

Love,
Gram
P.S. May god bless and keep you.
P.P.S. God will bless and keep you, I just know it!

Letters From Home

LETTER 07

Dear William,

Thank you so much for your last letter. You are the only one in the family that seems to have time for this old lady.

You will never guess who came to visit us the other day! Reverend Wilson! He was very apologetic and asked my forgiveness for his comments about you. He said that he couldn't sleep all that night, and turned as he always did, to scripture when he needed rest. He had been reading for some time in Leviticus, and had set the good book down because he had become a little drowsy, when a breeze came in the window, and turned the pages all the way to the New Testament. Imagine, such a wind!

He read where the Good Lord said judge not lest you be judged. He said that this got him to thinking. The Good Lord came here to help us, not make us hate each other. He said that we should all try to be better Christians by emulating Him, rather than judging one another, and he asked if your Grandfather and I would please come back to church. He said that you were of course welcome in the house of Our Lord, and that it was wrong of him to have ever said otherwise. I was so happy, I gave him an extra large chunk of my home-made cherry pie!

Well, Your Grandfather has gone down to the car dealership to look at their new line of automobiles. Although he never said so, I know he was glad to find out that you didn't need the extra money to be gay. I think he had his heart set on a new car. I'm not sure how we'll afford it, but it is so nice to see your Grandfather happy that I'm glad to tighten my belt a little if it means that he can have the car he wants.

Your brother stopped by to show me his new earring. Of course he wears it in his eyebrow. Since that is the style nowadays, I didn't say a word. But it was very distracting to talk to him. My eyes kept getting drawn up to his earring. He asked me what I thought of it, so I told him point blank that it was just fine with me. I bet you never thought your old Gram could be so hip!

Will close for now. William, please write to me. I enjoy your letters so much.

Love,
Gram
P.S. May god bless and keep you.

Letters From Home

LETTER 08

Dear William,

Thank you so much for your last letter. I have
some wonderful news!

Reverend Wilson preached a sermon about
not judging and forgiveness this past Sunday.
He mentioned you by name and told
everyone about what had happened! At first

everyone was very shocked about it all, but then they really started to listen. He said that people who quote scripture about the gays never quote the Good Lord who said that we should love one another as we want God to love us, and who said "that which you do to even the least of my brothers, that you do unto me."

Reverend Wilson asked us if we want to shut the Good Lord out of our Church, and everyone shouted NO! Then he said that we are all Christians, and it's high time we started acting like it! You should have been there! It was even better than his fire and brimstone sermons!

The Church council has decided to organize a bus trip to Provincetown, so we can all go there to find out about being gay. I told them to make sure they got the right Provincetown, and to be sure to get the one in Massachusetts and not the one in Rhode Island. It seems silly to have so many of them!

We are all very excited about the prospect, and hoping to see you as early as Labor Day! The house has turned into Grand Central Station. It seems like everyone in town has been coming over, since your Grandfather and I are "in-the-know" about Provincetown.

Please tell me exactly where it is, so we can make sure the bus driver gets it right!

I've been so busy making pies and cookies for all of our visitors, and keeping the house prepared for company that I almost have no time for myself. Your Grandfather spoke with the paperboy, and they have forgiven one another. The young man has even started bringing the Daily right to our door! Mrs. Babcock has been visiting quite a bit, and it seems I may have been mistaken about her interest in your Grandfather. She misses Mr. Babcock, and I think she may be lonely. She has been very helpful in entertaining our "drop-ins" and in helping me bake for all of them. She seems so much cheerier now.

Please write, you know we are always happy to hear from you.

Love,
Gram
P.S. May God Bless and Keep you.

Letters From Home

LETTER 09

Dear William,

I'm so sorry it's been so long since my last letter. I hope I haven't worried you! Things here have been so crazy lately what with the trip coming up and so many visitors at all hours of the day. I just don't have much time to write anymore. I hope you understand.

We have had to book a second bus for the trip this coming week. So many people have decided to join in, that it's going to seem like one big party. We are all so excited!

Your Brother came by the other day to show us his newest earring, which he wears in his bellybutton. I'm sorry, I'm trying to learn about these things, but it seems so silly to me. Why would you wear earrings in your belly button? I hope you don't think that I'm not still hip, but I imagine it must've hurt quite a bit. He seems very happy with it though, and I guess there's no harm done.

Your Grandfather is so happy now. You should see him. He washes his new car almost every day, and the neighbors go past waving. He waves back smiling so big you'd think his face was going to split in two. He even gave the paperboy a two-dollar tip the other day!

It really is amazing how just loving one another makes living so much easier. It seems we have so many more friends now. Your Grandfather hugged me the other day, for no reason at all! We got to talking, and have decided to renew our wedding vows in Provincetown! Your Grandfather wants you to be his best man! Will you do it? It will make him so happy. You know I will be happy just to see you again.

Well, have to close. The Church Council is coming over shortly to discuss the final plans for our trip. See you soon. Write if you can.

Love,
Gram
P.S. May God bless and keep you always.

Letters From Home

LETTER 10

Dear William,

What a lovely trip that was! We are all still buzzing about it, and what a lovely town you live in. We all voted and have decided to make it an annual event.

I'm so glad your Grandfather and I decided to have a commitment ceremony. It was so lovely! The flowers were so pretty and smelled so nice, and your boyfriend Robert was so kind to Mrs. Babcock that she nearly cried when it was time to go.

Your Grandfather and I were both so pleased to meet Robert. What a fine young man he is! So courteous and helpful. He reminded me of your Grandfather when I first met him. Of course your Grandfather wasn't gay, but still they have so many other similarities. Both so handsome and such gentlemen! Do we hear wedding bells???

You know, a man like Robert doesn't come along every day, William. I saw the way he was looking at you! He loves you very much. You know how happy your Grandfather and I have been, and we just want that same kind of happiness for you. We were all talking about it on the bus, and Mrs. Babcock said that the Government won't let you get married! Can that be true? We are all going to write letters to Congress and tell them we want them to fix their mistake right away. I'll sit at your wedding before the Good Lord takes me, or I'll know the reason why!

Oh, my goodness, I almost forgot to tell you. Your Brother has shaved his head and has two new earrings. He wears them in his ears, thank goodness! I think he expected us to be shocked when he met us at the bus station with that bald noggin of his. But he was the one shocked when I just kissed him on the top of the head and told him that sometimes, when you shave your head, the hair just doesn't grow back. You should have seen the look on his face.

Your Grandfather and I drifted off to sleep last night giggling about that.

You know, Christmas may seem very far away, but it isn't really. I hope you and Robert will come to stay with us over the holidays. It will be so nice to have you young folks over! We are both so proud of you, and we look forward to seeing you both soon.

Love,
Gram
P.S. May God Bless and keep you and Robert always.

Letters From Home

Letters From Home

.

www.ingramcontent.com/pod-product-compliance
Lightning Source LLC
Chambersburg PA
CBHW022134280326
41933CB00007B/688